Chinchín!

Cheers! Salut

Sláinte

Cheers!

L'chaim

Bravo

10 9 8 7 6 5 4 3 2 1

Vermilion, an imprint of Ebury Publishing
20 Vauxhall Bridge Road
London SW1V 2SA

Ebury Publishing is part of the Penguin Random House group of companies
whose addresses can be found at global.penguinrandomhouse.com

Penguin
Random House
UK

First published by Vermilion in 2016
www.penguin.co.uk

A CIP catalogue record for this book is availble from the British Library

Penguin Random House is commited to a sustainable future for our business,
our readers and our planet. This book is made from Forest Stewardship
Council® (FSC®), certified paper.

Printed and bound in China by Toppan Leefung

ISBN 9781785040795

UNACCUSTOMED AS I AM...
THE WEDDING SPEECH
MADE EASY

BY MICHAEL PARKER

To Eliza,
Laura and Hannah x :)

Michael Parker is the author of the bestselling book on how to present yourself when it really matters, 'It's not what you say, it's the way you say it!'

Having written numerous speeches, coached individuals in pitching and presentations, he is brilliantly equipped to share his tips, tricks and tools on delivering the best wedding speech ever. www.pitchcoach.co.uk

CONTENTS

ADVICE

BEAR IN MIND

COMPOSE IT

D-DAY DELIVERY

EXCEL YOURSELF

FOR EVERY ONE

ADVICE

'I ALWAYS PASS ON GOOD ADVICE. IT IS THE ONLY THING TO DO WITH IT. IT IS NEVER OF ANY USE TO ONESELF.'

OSCAR WILDE

'UNACCUSTOMED AS I AM...'

If you're giving a wedding speech, even if you're not one of the lucky couple, it's your Big Day too.

There's a lot of pressure on you. Where to start?

You can't wing it. It needs careful research and thought to decide just what it is that you want to say, to make it interesting and memorable. You will need to feel comfortable and relaxed about delivering it, so you will enjoy it as much as your audience.

While you are not yet a confident public speaker, you will find that the skills you practice naturally in everyday conversation are exactly what you need to make a winning speech.

'There are two types of speakers: those who get nervous and those who are liars.' **MARK TWAIN**

SEIZE THE DAY

One of the most well-known movie quotes was spoken by Robin Williams in *Dead Poets Society*: **'Carpe Diem, Seize the day, boys. Make your lives extraordinary.'**

Your speech may not change your life but it is a chance to do something extraordinary, a chance to enjoy showing off and to employ **kairos.**

Kairos is a classic rhetorical concept, used by many great orators, from Martin Luther King to Barack Obama, to capture in words the timeliness and the atmosphere of a particular moment.

Weddings are just such moments. Say the right thing for this particular moment in time and place and the audience will be yours.

**'*Thus though we cannot make our sun
Stand still, yet will we make him run.*'
Andrew Marvell**

IT'S A CELEBRATION!

Every moment of the Big Day is one of celebration.
It's an opportunity to congratulate and honour the happy couple,
show admiration and sing their praises.

Each speech may have a different role, but all will have at their
heart the spirit of praise and thanks, the feel-good factor.

Some guests, like the parents and bridesmaids, will be singled
out for special thanks and compliment, but everyone is part of
the celebration, part of making it a success, and all deserve a
pat on the back.

As a speaker you are helping capture the feelings and expressing
the good will felt by all.

The more personal your words, the more you will add to the celebration.

**'When people see your personality come out, they feel so good
like they actually know who you are.' USAIN BOLT**

YOU'RE THE ICING NOT THE CAKE

You will be in the spotlight when you speak but your speech is not a stand-alone event. It is just one of many ingredients which, after months of planning, go into making the day perfect.

Whichever speech you're making, (see For Everyone, p.130), you should ask the 'organiser' lots of questions:

Who else is speaking and what is the order?

Who do I thank, and who do I toast?

How long should my speech be?

Are there any specifics to be included?

Are there any 'don't go there' subjects?

Is there an overall theme for the day?

Can I see the guest list!

Asking the right questions early on will mean your speech being right for the occasion, right for the couple. After all it's their cake.

'Organising is what you do before you do something, so that when you do it, it is not all mixed up.' A.A.MILNE

THE WEDDING MAY
BE UNCONVENTIONAL...

Weddings around the world are steeped in traditions, some dating back thousands of years to the days of ancient Rome when the Bride wore a girdle that was tied in knots for the groom to grapple with later.

The knotted girdle may be long gone but a 'traditional' wedding remains the dream for many. For others, the dream is to create a wedding that breaks the mould.

...BUT THE PRINCIPLES OF SPEECHES ARE A CONSTANT

Whether formal or impromptu, religious or civil, straight or same sex, first, second, third or fourth marriage, at the heart is a constant: the celebration of the union of a couple.

And the basics of a good speech are a constant too. Depending on the nature of the event and the audience – hundreds of guests in a grand ballroom or a handful outside on a garden lawn – you may tailor the content of your speech, but stick to the principles.

'Tradition is a guide and not a jailer.'
W. SOMERSET MAUGHAM

BEAR IN MIND

'WE USE 10% OF OUR BRAINS. IMAGINE HOW MUCH WE COULD ACCOMPLISH IF WE USED THE OTHER 60%.'

ELLEN DEGENERES

FEEL THE LOVE

There are two types of speaker. One who gives the speech they want to give and one who gives the speech the audience wants to hear.

Aim to be the second kind.

Knowing what the audience wants at a Harry Potter convention, say, where everyone shares an interest, is pretty clear.

Your wedding guests, however, may be very diverse – culturally and socially and of all ages. But they all have one thing in common. They are there to celebrate the couple – to share the happiness.

They are not there to judge or criticize your speech. They will be willing you to succeed.

They are on your side.

'See, your guests approach. Address yourself to entertain them sprightly, And let's be red with mirth.'
WILLIAM SHAKESPEARE

PLAY THE GENERATION GAME

A generation is a span of twenty years or so and a wedding may have guests from five of them!

It is tempting to show off to your peers, who'll probably make up half of the crowd, getting laughs from an incident that means lots to them but little to others. But you should try to embrace the whole audience. It's best to sacrifice a little hilarity among your friends to make everyone feel included.

Win brownie points by engaging the little ones – children shouldn't be ignored or teenagers allowed to feel bored. Grandparents love to be acknowledged, and remember that parents are hanging on your every word.

Keep young and old in mind when writing your speech, but beware the ageism trap. We can all fall into it, as the old patronise the young and vice versa.

'There was no respect for youth when I was young and now that I'm old there is no respect for age – I missed it coming and going.' **J.B.PRIESTLEY**

MARRY THE TWO FAMILIES

Goodness knows what the mood would have been like at the wedding of Romeo and Juliet if they had invited their feuding families!

Hopefully it's not quite a case of Montagues vs Capulets at your wedding, but the two sides may have nothing in common apart from a connection to the couple. By focusing on the connection, your speech has the opportunity to unite the two households, however (un)alike they are in dignity.

You can make both sides feel even more at ease through use of **_ethos,_** another useful rhetorical concept. It calls for opening remarks that establish rapport, some common ground.

This can be acknowledgement, for example, that some will have crossed oceans to be there; of a shared interest in a popular news topic, or personality; even something as simple as the glorious/godawful weather.

'One love, one heart …
Let's get together and feel alright.' **BOB MARLEY**

WHAT'S IN A NAME?

People are proud of their names, its human nature. We like to be called by them and it makes us feel important. And yet in social situations, if shy or nervous, we are sometimes guilty of poor introductions. We stumble over a name, mispronounce it or worse still forget it.

Weddings are name fests! Guests are mingling and greeting or re-introducing themselves after years apart. And of course, there may be new name for one or both of the couple.

So, in your speech, name drop. Start by introducing yourself, warmly and with a smile, as you would at a party, telling them your name. It's an easy way to handle the 'difficult' first few words of your speech.

As you name the people you're here to thank, don't rush. Give 'space' to every name and if there are 10 bridesmaids, name and acknowledge each one, distinctly. All deserve it and will love being named.

A conscious delight in using names is a wonderful way of putting you at ease and of establishing a rapport with your audience.

'A person's name is to him or her the sweetest and most important sound in any language.' **DALE CARNEGIE**

THE EMBARRASSING QUESTION

Curiosity runs sky-high at a wedding. People meeting for the first time, linked only perhaps by knowing either the bride or the groom, expecting to find out who is who, what they are like. They look forward to hearing surprising truths and some secrets uncovered.

Your speech needs to play to their curiosity with the entertaining stories you tell. Being witty and funny is expected but don't make fools of the couple or their parents!

Try not to cross the line, and in deciding where that lies, remember the film *Four Weddings and a Funeral*. Something wildly funny to many was cringingly awful for a few.

It's tempting to go too far, so if unsure ask a friend for a good taste check.

'You can imagine my embarrassment when I killed the wrong guy.' JOE VALACHI, MAFIA

KEEP IT SHORT

History has forgotten Edward Everett, who spoke for two hours at Gettysburg in 1863. Abraham Lincoln's address afterwards lasted under three minutes. It changed the course of American history.

Even at the turn of the last century long wedding speeches had already 'fallen into disuse' (*Don'ts For Weddings*, 1904). Now, two to three minutes for the shorter speeches and seven or so for the longer 'Best Man' speech will do the trick.

Keep to the time agreed beforehand and don't fall into the trap of going 'off-piste', making things up as you go along. They liked that story, so I'll tell another one … and another … and …

Leave them wanting more!

'*Brevity is the soul of lingerie.*'
DOROTHY PARKER

COMPOSE IT

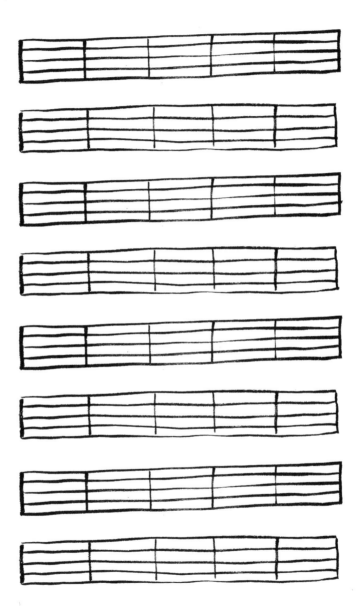

'THERE ARE THREE RULES FOR WRITING. UNFORTUNATELY, NO ONE CAN AGREE WHAT THEY ARE.'

W. SOMERSET MAUGHAM

START THINKING

Your speech may be months away or just a matter of weeks. Whichever, it's never too soon to start preparing. Procrastination puts you under pressure and can lead to needless nerves on the day.

Well before you start writing collect the raw material.

Mine your memory, making notes by topic, check 'records' on social media and old fashioned paper (school reports can be revealing), quiz friends and family for nuggets of insight or forgotten facts.

Talk to your 'subject' – the couple. While your speech is best as a surprise, ask them what they would like you to include. And what would they like you to avoid! Since it is their day, this is only fair.

A mind map will help make sense of the gathered material. It can save time and is an enjoyable way of sifting information and organising your thoughts. It can unlock possible themes and ideas.

To get started place put your subject at the centre with the main topics placed along the branches. Then have fun with the key words as the branches sub-divide.

'I try to prepare for everything beyond the extent of preparation.' TAYLOR SWIFT

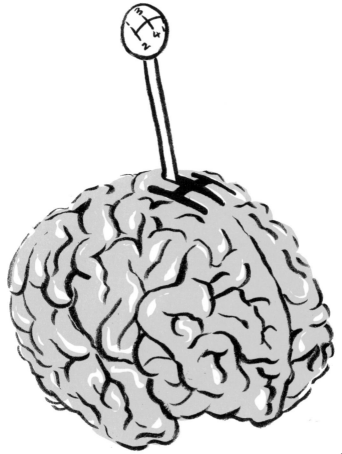

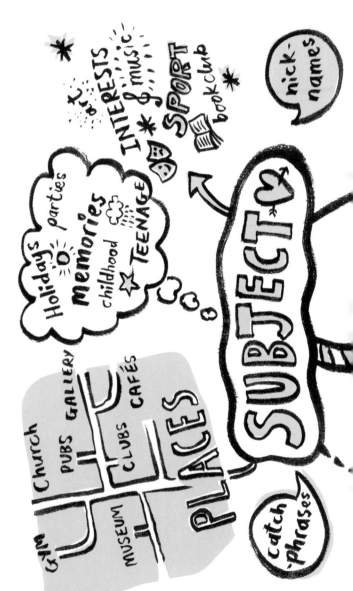

INCIDENTS »

Chance meeting
first date
blind date
trials ssss
& tribulations

WORK
Life

SCHOOL
COLLEGE
UNI
CAREER
PLACEMENTS
JOBS
PROMOTION
AWARDS

People:

parents
step-parents
Siblings

new friends
old friends

→ family

Aunts
Uncles
Cousins

neighbours

CHILDREN

Do-it-yourself

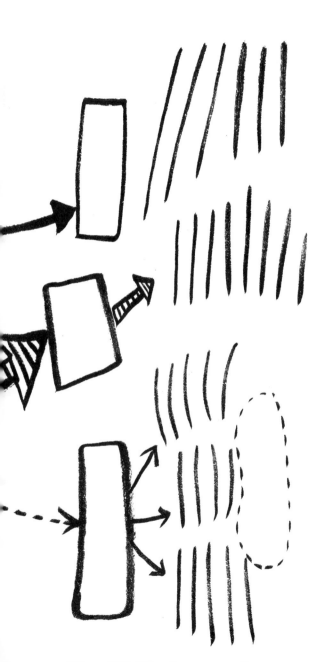

BEGIN BY SAYING THANK YOU!

The hardest part of any speech is the start. Any nerves you may have will be jangling. Your audience, many of them seeing you for the first time, will be at their most attentive. So crack the start and the rest will be downhill and easy.

And this is where the wedding speech gives you an advantage. You can start with a thank you.

Whichever speech you're making, you can find someone to thank for something!

Parents for a dutiful son or a beautiful daughter, bridesmaids for being supportive/ lovely, guests for braving bad weather, cousin Carol for the cake…

Single them out by name, thank them warmly and personally, then lead the applause.

Everyone will join in. It's a great feeling. They will be rooting for you even before you get into your speech. You will feel relieved, happy, even euphoric.

'I would maintain that thanks are the highest form of thought, and that gratitude is happiness doubled by wonder.'
G.K. CHESTERTON

TELL A STORY NOT A JOKE

It is easy to feel pressure, especially as Best Man or Best Woman, that your wedding speech has to be laugh-a-minute.

Cut yourself some slack! Not everyone is a natural comedian. And while you can source endless jokes from the internet, telling other people's jokes isn't easy.

Rather than overloading your speech with cheap gags that may fall flat, recount a few amusing stories about whoever it is you are toasting. You can create humour by the way you tell 'em.

Your audience will lap up personal stories and you will be on much safer ground if you let yourself off the hook of being a stand-up comic.

'I think being funny is not anyone's first choice.'
WOODY ALLEN

HANG IT BY A THREAD

This needs some time and thought, and maybe a bit of mind-mapping (page 56), to help you find the unique theme or thread of your whole speech. You will win points, of course, if it is something about the couple.

Rather than a random collection of stories and anecdotes, it will help to have your thread idea developing the narrative. As each story builds and expands on this, it will add interest and anticipation. Your speech will be even more memorable.

There is no magic formula for dreaming up your thread. Here are a few but it's your speech, enjoy being creative.

Milestones:
In his, her, their life or relationship

Places:
Significant in their journey

People:
Whose recollections help tell the story

List:
(6) things you didn't know about, ( )reasons why I like, love, admire…

Where, when, what, how:
Story of the romance unfolding

Central thought:
'Luck'/ 'destiny' / 'surprise'

Movie/book, adapted:
'Sleepless in Wolverhampton,' 'when Harry met … ,' pride and …'

'Where should I go?' – Alice
'That depends on where you want to end up'
– The Cheshire Cat
LEWIS CARROLL, ALICE IN WONDERLAND

WRITING YOUR SPEECH? IT'S AS EASY AS 1,2,3

Composing a longer speech can be daunting if your last serious writing was the school essay. Where to start? How to develop?

Life will be easier if you have a framework. One, often used by speakers, is known as the 'rule of three.' It means arranging the body of your speech, after introductions and thanks, into no more than three areas that develop your thread. (See previous page.)

For example, you might open with your thread as 'milestones in a romantic journey' and arrange your stories and anecdotes around 'early days', 'significant stops' and 'arrival'.

The idea of arrangement reflects Aristotle's three act plot structure in drama, typically: set-up; developing action; resolution.

Why not find your inner Shakespeare?

'… in the first act of a story you put your character up in a tree and the second act you set the tree on fire and then in the third you get them down.' BILLY WILDER

write to be
heard !

Generally we write to be read: school essays, university theses, business reports, texts and tweets, emails and emojis.

You alone will read your script. Everyone else will listen to it.

At the draft stage, write 'rough' and get down on paper the long uncorrected version of what you want to say.

Then create magic with editing. Trust your own ears. Keep reading aloud and let the words be guided by their sound.

Listen out for paragraphs that sound right and are not complicated. For sentences that are short and punchy.

Introduce some vivid adjectives but avoid the indecipherable that leads to mispronunciation.

Find phrases that are memorable and trip off the tongue.

Feeling adventurous? Try some repetition.

Feeling adventurous? Add alliteration.

Feeling adventurous? Ask a rhetorical question.

How do I love thee?
ELIZABETH BARRETT BROWNING

THE ART OF THE STORY

Humans are natural storytellers. They've been doing it for thousands of years. You do it all the time without thinking about it!

There's no more pressure on your storytelling abilities during your wedding speech than there is over dinner or in a bar with friends. The only difference is that nobody will talk over you, so you can take your time and really enjoy yourself.

It helps to keep storytelling casual and conversational as it will feel more intimate. Jot thoughts down as they occur to you and then assemble them at a later date rather than sitting down and forcing yourself to 'be inspired'. Be inclusive, make references that others will be familiar with. Play to your strengths.

Set the scene, lead the listener in and then end with a bang. The punchline needn't be funny, but it should be surprising or unexpected. You can do this by defying expectation: if you have been telling an irreverent story, with humour, end with sincerity.

'Great is the art of beginning, but greater is the art of ending.'
HENRY WADSWORTH LONGFELLOW

'THE FREEDOM OF POETIC LICENCE.'

CICERO

USE POETRY AS YOUR VOICE

There is no better time than a wedding to turn to poetry.

At its heart is a universal truth that unites us all and may not be possible to touch upon every day. On an occasion when feelings run high, poetry is able to open up the possibilities of expressing human emotion.

It can be grand, subtle, sweet, romantic, intimate and funny. As a speaker you needn't change tone for the sake of a poem, rather find a poem which fits with the overall tone you prefer for your speech.

'Poetry: the best words in the best order.'
SAMUEL TAYLOR COLERIDGE

PICK YOUR POEM

You can build your whole speech from something found within a poem, something that touches you or seems relevant to the wedding. Conversely, you can work from the thread you have already got in mind and find a poem to fit.

To do this, tailor your selection by looking at the intention of the poem. Consider the couple. Who are they? Literary? Passionate? Playful?

Ask them who their favourite writers are, whether there is a poem, book or even a song that is special to them and use that as a springboard for your research.

Then there's you. Can you be sincere? Funny? Don't try and use poetry that you are not comfortable delivering.

'The world is never the same once a good poem has been added.' DYLAN THOMAS

Roses are red,
violets are blue,
This selection of poems
Might be useful to you

A SELECTION OF POETS AND POETRY

The 'classic' poets used at weddings are well known.

Shakespeare of course, and a one line reminder of others:

'You can give without loving…' from *Les Miserables*,

'So, we'll go no more a-roving.' Lord Byron is often used, and

'How do I love thee?' by Elizabeth Barrett Browning.

'Come live with me and be my love' Christopher Marlowe

'Love is patient, love is kind' 1 Corinthians 13

Here are some poems with the intentions of the poets which might help you choose one suited to your speech.

Rilke — *sincere, heartfelt*

Love Song:

Understand, I'll slip quietly
Away from the noisy crowd
When I see the pale
Stars rising, blooming over the oaks.
I'll pursue solitary pathways
Through the pale twilit meadows,
With only this one dream:
You come too.

Elizabeth Bishop — *elegant, witty*

Close, close all night:

Close, close all night
the lovers keep.
They turn together
in their sleep,
close as two pages
in a book
that read each other
in the dark.

Pablo Neruda *– intimate, passionate*

From Your Feet:

But I love your feet
only because they walked
upon the earth and upon
the wind and upon the waters,
until they found me.

John Cooper Clarke *– funny, irreverent, punk*

I wanna be yours:

I wanna be your vacuum cleaner
Breathing in your dust
I wanna be your Ford Cortina
I will never rust
If you like your coffee hot
Let me be your coffee pot
You call the shots
I wanna be yours

Kahlil Gibran *– philosophical, humble*

On Marriage:

Love one another, but make not a bond of love:
Let it rather be a moving sea between the shores of your souls.
Fill each other's cup but drink not from one cup.
Give one another of your bread but eat not from the same loaf
Sing and dance together and be joyous,
but let each one of you be alone,
Even as the strings of a lute are alone though
they quiver with the same music.

Maya Angelou *– joyful, spiritual*

Touched by an Angel:

We are weaned from our timidity
In the flush of love's light
we dare be brave
And suddenly we see
that love costs all we are
and will ever be.
Yet it is only love
which sets us free.

Jane Hirshfield *– spiritual, tender*

A Blessing for a Wedding

Today, let this light bless you
With these friends let it bless you
With snow-scent and lavender bless you
Let the vow of this day keep itself wildly and wholly
Spoken and silent, surprise you inside your ears
Sleeping and waking, unfold itself inside your eyes
Let its fierceness and tenderness hold you
Let its vastness be undisguised in all your days

E.E. Cummings *– sweet, pithy*

I carry your heart

i carry your heart with me(i carry it in
my heart)i am never without it(anywhere
i go you go,my dear;and whatever is done
by only me is your doing, my darling)

Michael Donaghy *– erudite, playful*

The Present

Forget the here-and-now. We have no time
but this device of wantonness and wit.
Make me this present then: your hand in mine,
and we'll live out our lives in it.

Margaret Atwood *– mythical, unsentimental*

Variations on the Word Love

This word is not enough but it will
have to do. It's a single
vowel in this metallic
silence, a mouth that says
O again and again in wonder
and pain, a breath, a finger
grip on a cliffside. You can
hold on or let go.

THE POETRY READING

Warm your audience up to the idea of the poem and why you have chosen it.

Read holding the book containing the poem. This works better than a slip of paper – it doesn't betray a shaking hand, it adds a touch of gravitas and you're less likely to lose it on the day.

Now to delivering the poem:

Firstly, familiarise yourself with it. This is especially important if it is a poem your audience is likely to have heard before. It ensures you're not just reciting it as if it were a times table, but delivering it with understanding. The more used you are to speaking the poem out loud, the more naturally you will be able to deliver it.

Read slowly. Slower than that! Give the text space to breathe. Allow the meaning of each line to be absorbed before moving onto the next. Make notes in the margins to remind you to take a breath, or to pause more dramatically.

Underline words that require stress and remind yourself to look up at your audience occasionally…

Have fun. This poem means something to you and is important to the occasion. Lucky audience that they get to hear it!

'If you cannot be a poet, be the poem.'
DAVID CARRADINE

MAKE IT MEMORABLE

Your speech will be a success if a) the couple enjoy it, b) the guests enjoy it and c) you enjoy it! The ideas in this book will help you achieve all three.

You may want to go further, making the speech that gets talked about and is remembered. On a day when lots of other memories are formed this is not easy but is an enjoyable challenge.

Here are a few pointers:

In any speech the strong emotional story wins the memory test.

The clever, witty phrase used repeatedly will stand out.

Pictures paint a thousand words. Use one where the venue allows.

Feeling brave? Stand on a table.

You could invite a guest, apparently spontaneously, to add their take to a story you are telling.

In short, be imaginative and look for the unexpected ideas but keep in mind it's their enjoyment not your brilliance that matters.

'The happiest conversation is that of which nothing is remembered, but a general effect of pleasing impression.'
TAYLOR SWIFT

END ON A HIGH NOTE

In any speech you want to end bringing the audience to their feet in appreciation. Here you have an advantage since you will be asking them to stand for a toast. (Whichever speech you give, there is usually someone who deserves to be recognised, from the couple to absent friends.)

To build anticipation, your final words before the toast should set out to raise the temperature. Perhaps with a strong quote that captures the sentiment, or the repetition of a key thought, or the ending of a poignant anecdote.

Pause for dramatic effect. (Check you have your glass filled.)

Then in naturally very personal words ask everyone to stand and join you in wishing whoever you are toasting – looking directly at them – every possible future happiness.

These last words, like your opening ones, you should memorise. This frees you from looking down at your notes. You can just be yourself, letting your emotions take over. So don't hold back. Go for it.

'Feelings are important. Emotions are important.
I'm not just an emoji, even though I live in that age.'
LADY GAGA

D-DAY DELIVERY

'STAND UP STRAIGHT AND REALIZE WHO YOU ARE, THAT YOU TOWER OVER YOUR CIRCUMSTANCES.'

MAYA ANGELOU

ENJOY THE MOMENT

Your speech is a performance and, as actors will tell you, the more you can be 'in the moment' the more you will enjoy it. And this is an occasion to enjoy!

Put another way it's about staying in the present. Your focus is on sharing your feelings about something that means a lot to you, rather than worrying about your audience's reaction.

You need to get into the mind-set of 'it's not what you say, it's the way you say it.' Feeling good about yourself in what is a challenging moment will lift your performance. And preparation and delivery practice will make all the difference.

While some nervous anticipation is the norm, you should have every reason to feel relaxed and confident. You love the people you're talking about, you believe in what you are saying and your passion will carry the day!

So enjoy. The more you can be yourself, the more present you'll be. And people will listen, not judge!

'Forever is composed of nows.' **EMILY DICKINSON**

x_3 $B_{\#}$

$$x = \frac{-b \pm \sqrt{b^2 - 4ac}}{2a}$$

$A \sim 10^{10}\,(10^{11})\,\mathrm{J}$

$P \sim 10^8\,\mathrm{y} \cdot \mathrm{J}$

$$x^2 + \frac{b}{a}x + \frac{c}{a} = 0$$

$\rho \sim 10^{-26}$

$$x^2 + \frac{b}{a}x + \left(\frac{b}{2a}\right)^2 = -\frac{c}{a} + \left(\frac{b}{2a}\right)^2$$

$$\pi_{\mu\nu} = \frac{8\pi G}{c^4}\,T_{\mu\nu}$$

$$x = \frac{b}{2a} \pm \sqrt{b^2}$$

$G_{\mu\nu}$

$$\begin{matrix} 1 & 0 & 0 & 0 \\ 0 & 1 & 0 & 0 \\ 0 & 0 & 1 & 0 \end{matrix}$$

$$x = \frac{3 \pm \sqrt{(-3)^2 - 4(2)(1/2)}}{2(2)} = \frac{3}{}$$

$$D^2 = \frac{1}{p^2}\,\frac{P_0 - P}{P} \sim \frac{1}{p^2} \quad (1a)$$

$$W^{m+1} = \frac{1}{T}\sum_{i=0}^{i_a} \frac{(1-w)\,f_2\,(i-1/\lambda_2{}^m)\,y\,(a+i)(i-1)}{w^m\,f_1\,(i|\lambda_1{}^m) + (1-w)^m\,f_2\,(i-1|\lambda_2{}^m)}$$

$$E^2 = m^2 c^4 + p^2 c^2$$

Preparation + Rehearsal
= CONFIDENCE !

$$)^2 = \frac{K\rho}{3}\,\frac{P_0 - P}{P} \sim \sqrt[4]{K\rho}$$

$\left(\dfrac{b}{2a}\right)^2$ $\quad D^2 \sim 10^{-53}$

A QUESTION OF CONFIDENCE

You will enjoy the moment more as you gain confidence.

Even professional platform speakers experience a degree of nervousness, it's natural. In fact, science (Yerkes-Dodson Principle) demonstrates the positive relationship: a certain amount of stress – not too much – is healthy, useful and beneficial. It can inspire you to perform well.

The caveat is that you must prepare!

You need to trust the work you do in preparation for the 'special' moment. If you have trust in all the work you have done, this will translate to your feeling on stage (or table).

The next page explores the practical preparation you can take. Put simply, the more you rehearse, the more you will keep your stress level in check and the more you will embrace and look forward to speaking.

'If you're presenting yourself with confidence, you can pull off pretty much anything.' **KATY PERRY**

CONQUER ... UH ... UH ... THE NERVES

Five practical steps to keep stress in check.

1. Break your speech into bite-size chunks – each no more than one to three minutes – making it easier to deliver.

2. Master the start. Your first words are the hardest. Make them short and easy to say. Memorise them, if nothing else. No jokes.

3. Follow your signposts. The key words that keep you on track and reduce the need for notes (see page 106.)

4. Rehearse to someone! Get them to judge your performance, and the more you do it, the less nervous you'll be.

5. Practice your pauses. Pause to breathe deeply, for thought. Pauses make you seem confident and they help your confidence.

'I get nervous when I don't get nervous. If I'm nervous I know I'm going to have a good show.' **BEYONCE**

IT'S NOT JUST A SPACE, IT'S A STAGE

Actors learn early on how to 'own' their stage – how to enter it, where to stand, how to use space to enhance their performance.

You should do all you can to own your space.

In some weddings a formal rehearsal will give you the opportunity. Otherwise find time before you speak, as an actor would, to check that the 'space' allocated is right for you. If it's not, change it.

Don't speak squeezed between seated guests, or from the wrong end of a table, or hidden behind a flower arrangement, or a pillar, or the far corner of a marquee. Avoid towering above on a too-high platform or sheltering behind a formidable lectern. Your audience want to feel you are sharing not lecturing!

What matters is that you feel comfortable in your space. It should allow you to move freely. It should allow your audience to see and hear you easily. It is your speech, your stage.

'When I'm on stage, all is right with the world.'
GLORIA GAYNOR

TAKE A DEEP BREATH

If you practice yoga you'll know all about the way breathing correctly can calm the nerves and make you feel powerful. Exactly what will help you handle your speech without fear!

Ideally, you should learn – there are good online sources – and start practicing 'breathing and speaking,' well in advance of your speech. Failing this the least you can do is focus on your breathing before you get up to speak.

If you are sitting take a moment to plant your feet firmly on the floor. As you breathe in allow the inhalation to expand your diaphragm and fill your lungs. As you breathe out allow your body to relax and you will feel confident, grounded, and ready!

It's hard to remember to breathe during your speech if you haven't practiced, so don't worry if you've not mastered it. Try, consciously, to breathe when you pause (page 112). And certainly take a few steady deep breaths before you start.

You will feel calmer and your voice will sound warmer and stronger.

'I've got to keep breathing. It'll be my worst business mistake if I don't.' STEVE MARTIN

YOUR CHANCE TO SHINE

When you stand up to speak the guests will form an instant impression of you. They can't help it. Before you say a word your body will be talking! And you want it to say the right things.

Given there are, apparently, 7,000 different signs and facial expressions, deciding which to adopt could be daunting. Fortunately you don't need to.

In her brilliant TED Talk, Amy Cuddy shows that you can 'fake it till you become it.' You decide the mood you want to feel in yourself, the one you want to come across, (happy, eager, optimistic, confident), and then practice the appropriate body language.

Do this for a few minutes, away from everyone, before you speak. Walk with a swagger, enjoy filling your lungs, punch the air, keep your head high, your shoulders back, smile inanely in a mirror, take up a power pose. Try it now. It works.

How? As the body can shape the mind, which in turn shapes your behaviour, open expansive body language decreases feelings of stress while increasing feelings of optimism and happiness. Just what you need for the celebration.

'I speak two languages, Body and English.' MAE WEST

R
EA
DING
IS BAD
FOR YOUR EYES

LOOK OUT

It is tempting, if you're speaking for the first time, to look for the reassurance of reading from your script. Try not to be tempted.

You should aim to be looking up and out because, if you read, your eyes look down, 'dismissing' your audience. They want to feel you are sharing your thoughts with them and will find listening difficult if there is no eye contact. Reading inhibits your body language too, and your smile, reducing your spontaneity and naturalness, things your audience look for.

It is also tempting to think that memorising until you are word perfect will work. Again, avoid this. If your speech becomes a recital it will seem stilted and forced. It takes a skilled actor to deliver learned lines with emotion.

For most, the best practical approach is to prepare, and then practice, with 'signpost' notes (following page). These can keep you on track if the need arises. If you want a reminder, pause to glance at them, then look up and continue talking. Trick is not to speak while reading.

'The face is a picture of the mind with the eyes as its interpreter.'
CICERO

WITHOUT SIGNPOSTS YOU'RE LOST

Better than reading or memorising your speech, you will find that 'signpost' notes will help you speak naturally and confidently.

When you are happy with your script, break it down into chunks and assign each main thought a signpost word or phrase. In a five minute speech you may need ten, no more.

For example, if your speech thread involves milestone events, then signposts like the 'Anchor pub', or 'Devon weekend' will trigger all you wanted to say. If you have several people to thank, make each name a signpost. 'Happy accident' will put you in story telling mode.

Put your signposts on cards, with large type, easy to hold and to read. Practice using them, talking out loud. At first you may need frequent prompting, but don't read and talk at same time. You should pause, then glance, then look up and go on talking.

After a while, you will not really need the signposts at all. You know the way. Having them is like a security blanket that allows you to feel free in expressing yourself.

As with any security system, don't use unless you have to!

IF MUSIC BE THE FOOD OF LOVE

Barack Obama's best speeches have a musicality to them. That's because his speechwriters obsess over rhythm and cadence. They understand how variations in pitch and pace, volume and tone lend expression to his voice.

Mastering all of these takes time but that is no reason why you should be a 'Johnny one-note'. Try breaking your speech into phases, as if it was a musical score, each with its *tempo* notation.

Your opening 'hello and thank you' should be brisk, cheerful and lively, *allegro*, leading to the body of your speech, the stories and memories where your tone is *scherzo*, playful and light.

Expressing your feelings of love or admiration will be a present moment, serious but impassioned, **declamando**, before a spirited, fiery **con brio** toast as your finale.

Like the musician, practice your tempo in rehearsal.

'The human voice is the most beautiful instrument of all, but it is the most difficult to play.' RICHARD STRAUSS

Now that you've done your homework on the guests, got your speech idea and the words working together thought of some stories and anecdotes, selected quotes or a poem, know who it is you have to thank and who you are to toast, timed yourself and are ready to rehearse properly, there's one last ingredient which will make a vast difference, wait for it, …

… the magic of …

...the pause

If there is one thing you can do, above all else, to bolster your confidence and enjoy making your speech, it is to pause.

This does not call for changing your speed of talking, which is tough to do. It is simply practising what you do naturally in everyday conversation – when you pause for thought, pause to check you are understood and pause for emphasis.

Debussy said **'Music is the space between the notes.'**
For you, your speech will happen in the pauses.

Make their magic work for you ...

… to grab attention before you start, *pause;* before and after saying 'thank you,' *pause;* to separate the parts of your speech, *pause;* to emphasise key phrases, *pause;* to add drama to your stories, *pause;* to slow you down, *pause;* to take a breath, *pause;* to sip a glass of water, *pause;* to allow (distracted) guests to 'catch up,' *pause;* to be seen to be thoughtful, *pause;* to calm your nerves, *pause;* to control your voice, *pause;* to set up anticipation of your toast, *pause;* to look, and feel, more confident, *pause;* to smile, *pause.*

Even if you are unaccustomed, mastering the pause is the easiest and quickest way to feeling more at ease when you give your speech.

'The right word may be effective, but no word was ever as effective as a rightly timed pause'. **MARK TWAIN**

EXCEL YOURSELF

'I AM ALWAYS DOING THAT WHICH I CANNOT DO, IN ORDER THAT I MAY LEARN HOW TO DO IT.'

PABLO PICASSO

REHEARSAL, TAKE ONE, TAKE TWO, TAKE THREE

When you stand to speak, you'll be in the spotlight performing in front of your audience. To be at your confident best then, like an actor, you need to rehearse and you'll need someone to rehearse to, someone to direct you.

Rehearsal is all about what your audience will take out, not what you put in.

Find a friend, your director, to act as your audience. Their role is not to critique the speech content, but to tell you how you come across. Do this in your venue if possible, or a similar space.

It will help to rehearse chunks of your speech separately, gradually becoming less dependent on your signpost notes. Then you can go through the entire speech, gaining assurance each time you do it.

Rehearsing may feel embarrassing at first, but each time you do it your confidence will grow.

'All the world's a stage and most of us are desperately unrehearsed.'
SEÁN O'CASEY

GET A SENSE OF DIRECTION

Was I 'standing tall' and not rooted to the spot?

Did I vary the tempo, the pace?

Could I be heard easily at the back of the room?

Was I totally at ease with my (learnt) opening words?

Was my energy level up throughout?

Did I tell my stories well?

Was I pausing … enough?

Was I looking up, or down?

Were there any tricky phrases or distractions?

Did I finish on a high note?

Was I at my smiling, charming best?

**'*Have more than you show, speak less than you know.*'
WILLIAM SHAKESPEARE, *KING LEAR***

I do...

… follow my speaker's brief

… start preparing early

… check out the venue

… rehearse to someone neutral

… keep it personal and natural

… know who I must thank

… memorise my opening words

… have a thread to follow

… find humour in my stories

… breathe deeply before I start

… stand tall to feel tall

… look up, look out

… trust my signposts

… remember to … pause

… toast enthusiastically

… smile

I don't...

… leave my precious notes behind

… think a drink will make me a hero

… say anything to upset anyone

… read my speech, eyes down

… talk longer than was agreed!

… try to tell jokes when I can't

… fidget with hair, keys or coins

… put hands in pocket or behind back

… stand immobile like a statue

… over-react to rowdy guests

… speak if I can't be seen or heard

… use hard-to-pronounce words

… forget the names that matter

… hold back my feelings

… forget to smile

TRIVIA TO TRIFLE WITH

The custom of the bride standing on the left of the groom is rooted in his need for his sword arm to be free for action.

After Teutonic weddings, only held under the full moon, bride and groom drank honey wine for one full moon cycle. This 'month' became known as the honey moon.

In 16th century London a law forbade wife-beating after 9pm but only because the noise disturbed people's sleep.

The word 'wedding' comes from the Anglo-Saxon word *wedd* that meant a man would marry a woman and pay the Bride's father.

The most expensive wedding gift of all time is the cities of Tangiers and Bombay (given to Queen Luisa of Portugal by Charles II of England in 1659).

In medieval England, cakes were washed down with a special ale, bryd ealu, translated as 'bride's ale' that became the word bridal.

Ancient Greeks used pig entrails to determine the luckiest day to marry. In early U.S. history Wednesday was the luckiest day. Friday was avoided as the 'hangman's day.'

The Anglo Saxon father saw marriage as a way of expanding the labour force and would use his daughter as a form of currency to pay off debts or buy his way into a higher social status.

Bachelor parties in French-speaking countries are still known as *l'enterrement de vie de garçon*, the burial of the life as a boy.

Mutual attraction in marriage was not important until late 18th century. In fact in Victorian England, many held that women didn't have strong sexual urges.

In ancient Rome, bridesmaids and groomsmen were decoys who dressed alike to confuse evil spirits who might target the bride and groom.

2,000 years ago the best man's role was more than just safeguarding the ring. Well-armed, he remained at the grooms side to fight the real threat that the bride's family would attempt to obtain her return by force.

In the Crying Ritual in the Sichuan Province, China, starting 30 days before the wedding, the bride spends an hour a day crying. Ten days later, she is joined by her mother, and then ten days after that her grandmother. It's a sign of joy.

Engagement and wedding rings are worn on the 4th finger of the left hand because it was thought that the vena amori, vein of love, led directly to the heart.

The role of wives as 'peace weavers' was crucial in containing the clan rivalries that were rampant in Germanic and Viking societies.

The ancient Greeks thought lovesickness was a type of insanity while the French in the Middle Ages defined love as 'a sickness of the mind' that could be cured by sexual intercourse – with the loved one or a different partner!

In New England a man could be whipped or imprisoned if he 'inveigled' or 'insinuated' himself into a woman's affections without her parents consent to the courtship.

The term marriage comes from the Latin word *mas* meaning 'male' or 'masculine.' The earliest known use of the word in English dates from the 13th century.

Byzantine rulers often selected their wives at a 'bride show' that resembled a modern beauty pageant.

An American advice book of the 1940s summed up two decades of dating advice to women asserting that the average man 'will go as far as you will let him go.'

George Bernard Shaw described marriage as an institution that brings together two people 'under the influence of the most violent, most insane, most delusive, and most intransient of passions. They are required to swear that they will remain in that excited, abnormal and exhausted condition continuously until death do them part.'

In the 1400s and 1500s most took their yearly communal bath in May and married by June while still smelling pretty good. Possibly the reason brides started carrying bouquets was to hide the body odour.

Bride kidnapping has been around since the founding of Rome, rife in England until the Marriage Act, 1753, and still practiced in countries like Kyrgyzstan, with the custom of *ala kachuu*, 'grab and run'.

FOR EVERYONE

Great Auntie
friends
All faiths
siblings
Grand Parents
neighbours
best men
Estranged
partners
mother of bride
father of bride
Mother of groom
colleagues
betrothed
culture

'ALL THE WORLD'S A STAGE, AND ALL THE MEN AND WOMEN MERELY PLAYERS.'

WILLIAM SHAKESPEARE

WHO SPEAKS ABOUT WHOM?

The answer is in the gift of the couple. It's their day after all. What part do they want speeches to play?

How will they add to the occasion? What are the expectations of their guests? How many speeches and for how long? Who should speak?

For many 'tradition' will be the guide but what matters is who do they feel is right to star in their show.

Once selected, what each speaker says will be dictated largely by their own personal experiences and feelings, expressed through reminiscence and stories.

The way to approach any speech has been explored earlier. In terms of specific content to cover, it helps to follow a template (next page) of the elements common to most speeches. You can tailor your own thread and words around the elements.

The template is demonstrated in a 60 second speech designed to cover everything. For example, where time is short and only one person speaks.

'Who in the world am I? Ah, that's the great puzzle.'
LEWIS CARROLL, *ALICE IN WONDERLAND*

THE
WEDDING
RECEPTION
OF THE YEAR

STARRING

THE GENEROUS HOSTS
(MOTHER - FATHER - OR FRIEND)

THE WORLDS HAPPIEST COUPLE
(THE GROOM OR BRIDE OR BOTH)

BEST OF THE BEST
BEST MAN AND/OR BEST WOMAN

BEST OF THE REST
(BRIDESMAIDS & GROOMSMEN)

BY INVITATION
SPECIAL GUEST OR RELATIVE

THE IMPROMPTU
THE SURPRISE SPEAKER

MASTER OF CEREMONIES

THE 60 SECOND
SPEECH DEMONSTRATION

WELCOME

INTRODUCE

THANKS

COMPLIMENTS

RELATIONSHIP

TOAST

NAMES

Good afternoon everyone! *pause* and welcome to this very special day. *pause*

My name is **Z**, *pause* and I'm speaking as a long term friend of both **X** and **Y**. *pause*

Thank you all for coming today and thank you, our generous hosts, for your wonderful hospitality. *pause to lead applause*

I have known **X** since school, a loyal friend, one of the brightest, kindest people you could meet. *pause*
Y is, quite simply, charm personified.

pause They met two years ago and it was love at first sight!
pause

Please raise your glasses and join me in wishing **X** and **Y** a fabulous future together.

pause to raise glasses **To X and Y!!!**

THE PARENTS OR HOSTS

Traditionally, the father of the bride carried the cost and spoke first. Today the cost may be borne by the couple, their parents or friends.

The 'host' speech is usually by one parent, but can be two, or a friend.

Use the 60 second demo as your guide. **Thank** guests for coming, (some a long way), **thank** people who have contributed to the day.

Compliment and praise your daughter, or son, with a story perhaps.

Express your delight about the **relationship,** welcoming and **complimenting** the new member of your family.

Make the key **toast** of the day to the happy future of the couple.

'I don't think my parents liked me. They put a live teddy bear in my crib.' **WOODY ALLEN**

THE COUPLE

Traditionally the groom spoke for the couple. Today it will be the bride or the groom, or both can speak separately. Their choice!

They can 'box and cox' a joint speech, which can be fun. Rehearsal is key to make sure the speeches don't clash, and you are seen as 'one'.

This speech has a lot of **thanks** in it. Definitely **thanks** to the first speaker for their kind words. You should thank everyone for their gifts.

Thanking all the parents (for everything) is a good idea, and **thanking** anyone else who deserves it. Talk about your relationship.

You will certainly want to **compliment** your new wife or husband and finish, traditionally, with **thanks** and a **toast** to the bridesmaids.

'In Hollywood, brides keep the bouquets and throw away the groom.' **GROUCHO MARX**

THE BEST MAN OR BEST WOMAN

The best man, best woman, or sometimes best men and women, speech is often longer and fills the entertainment slot.

Start with more **welcomes.** Repeating some won't hurt.

Thanks may be due on behalf of the bridesmaids. Or anyone left out.

Through light-hearted story-telling and personal experience say (mainly) **complimentary** things about the groom or the bride, or both.

Reveal surprising insights into the **relationship,** how they met, how it blossomed, how it is now and perhaps offer advice for their future.

You may need to read out cards, snapchats, even tweets, but finish with heartfelt congratulations, **toasting** the newly-weds.

'You mustn't upstage the bride.'
IAN MCKELLEN

BEST OF THE REST

Couples can ask bridesmaids, groomsmen, relatives, friends or special guests to speak. Guest attention span is the main consideration.

With more speakers, agreeing a brief – who **toasts** whom, in what order and for how long – is essential. Keep to time agreed.

Use the 60 second demo to guide you. The need to **introduce** yourself is greater with more speakers. You may **thank** different people, as well as hosts.

Compliments, praise, stories told and any **relationship** advice will be personal but try to check you are not duplicating other speakers.

'*Be sincere, be brief: be seated.*'
FRANKLIN D. ROOSEVELT

THE IMPROMPTU SPEAKER

When Plan B operates a last minute speaker may be needed. Or a well-meaning guest, un-asked, may volunteer a few words.

Both should keep it very brief. Speaking off the cuff is a rare skill, with nerves and/or champagne.

Unprepared, you may fall into the 'offending ' trap. Avoid religion, politics, resist the risqué, if in doubt don't say it.

Stick to the 60 second speech guide and aim to keep your spontaneous contribution to no more than two minutes.

'I never could make a good impromptu speech without several hours to prepare it.' **MARK TWAIN**

MASTER OF CEREMONIES OR A STAND-IN

Couples may assign this role to a 'professional', or to a best man or woman. Ask them to be responsible for managing the speakers.

MC or a stand-in may introduce the speakers on the day.

Will make sure they know the order of speaking, how long they have, agreeing who thanks who for what, and who they will toast.

If there are several speakers, with a light touch guide them from too much overlapping content. It is not his or her job to act as censor.

If the guests need managing, the MC can step in!

'An MC is somebody who can control the crowd. An MC is a master of ceremonies so not only can you say your rap, you can rock the party.' **ICE T**

WHY QUOTE A QUOTE?

'I love quotations because it is a joy to find thoughts one might have, beautifully expressed with much authority by someone recognized wiser than oneself.' **MARLENE DIETRICH**

LOVER TO LOVER

'How do I love thee? Let me count the ways.
I love thee to the depth and breadth and height My soul can reach.'
Elizabeth Barrett Browning

'He's more myself than I am. Whatever our souls are made of, his and mine are the same.'
Emily Brontë

'It was only a sunny smile, and little it cost in the giving, but like morning light it scattered the night and made the day worth living.'
F. Scott Fitzgerald

'The future for me is already a thing of the past —
You were my first love and you will be my last.'
Bob Dylan

'If you live to be 100, I hope I live to be 100 minus 1 day, so I never have to live without you.'
A.A. Milne, *Winnie the Pooh*

'I love thee – I love thee! Tis all that I can say;
It is my vision in the night, My dreaming in the day.'
Thomas Hood

'The only way you can beat my crazy was by doing something crazy yourself. Thank you. I love you. I knew it the minute I met you. I'm sorry it took so long for me to catch up. I just got stuck.'
The Silver Linings Playbook

'I'm in you and you in me, mutual in divine Love.'
William Blake

'If I loved you less, I might be able to talk about it more.'
Jane Austen

'If I know what love is, it is because of you.'
Hermann Hesse

'The heart wants what it wants. There's no logic to these things. You meet someone and you fall in love and that's that.'
Woody Allen

'You are the finest, loveliest, tenderest, and most beautiful person I have ever known and even that is an understatement.'
F. Scott Fitzgerald

'If I had a flower for every time I thought of you ... I could walk through my garden for ever.'
Alfred Tennyson

'I see you everywhere, in the stars, in the river: to me you're everything that exists; the reality of everything.'
Virginia Woolf

ALL ABOUT LOVE

'Love is the greatest refreshment in life.'
Pablo Picasso

'Love recognises no barriers. It jumps hurdles, leaps fences, penetrates walls to arrive at its destination.'
Maya Angelou

'Love is a canvas furnished by Nature and embroidered by imagination.'
Voltaire

'Keep love in your heart. A life without it is like a sunless garden when the flowers are dead.'
Oscar Wilde

'One word frees us of all the weight and pain of life: That word is love.'
Sophocles

'Nobody has ever measured, not even poets, how much the heart can hold.'
Zelda Fitzgerald

'The best thing to hold onto in life is each other.'
Audrey Hepburn

'Love is the joy of the good, the wonder of the wise, the amazement of the Gods.'
Plato

'Love is trembling happiness.'
Khalil Gibran

'How do you spell 'love'?' - Piglet
'You don't spell it … you feel it.' - Pooh
A.A. Milne

'Seize the moments of happiness, love and be loved!
That is the only reality in the world, all else is folly.'
Leo Tolstoy

'Love is our true destiny. We do not find the meaning of life by
ourselves alone – we find it with another.'
Thomas Merton

'In our life there is a single colour, as on an artist's palette, which
provides the meaning of life and art. It is the colour of love.'
Marc Chagall

'It matters not who you love, where you love, why you love, when
you love or how you love, it matters only that you love. '
John Lennon

'You don't love someone for their looks, or their loathes or their
clothes or for their fancy car, but because they sing a song only
your heart can hear.'
Oscar Wilde

'Love doesn't make the world go round, love is what makes the
ride worthwhile.'
Elizabeth Barrett Browning

LOVE BITES

'The course of true love never did run smooth.'
William Shakespeare

'Longed for him. Got him. Shit.'
Margaret Atwood

'Men and women, women and men. It will never work.'
Erica Jong

'Men marry women with the hope they will never change. Women marry men with the hope they will change. Invariably they are both disappointed.'
Albert Einstein

'Marriage is the most advanced form of warfare in the modern world.'
Malcolm Bradbury

'Dammit, sir, it is your duty to get married. You can't be always living for pleasure.'
Oscar Wilde

'The trouble with some women is that they get all excited about nothing – and then they marry him!'
Cher

'What the world really needs is more love and less paperwork.'
Pearl Bailey

'She gave me a smile I could feel in my hip pocket.'
Raymond Chandler

'She rocks my world.'
David Beckham

'Woman was God's second mistake.'
Friedrich Nietzsche

'The longest sentence you can form with two words is 'I do.''
H.L. Mencken

'Love is a game that two can play and both win.'
Eva Gabor

'After all these years I see that I was mistaken about Eve in the beginning; it is better to live outside the Garden with her than inside it without her.'
Mark Twain, *The Diaries of Adam & Eve*

'Of all the gin joints, in all the towns, in all the world,
She had to walk into mine.'
Casablanca

'Marge, you're as pretty as Princess Leia and as smart as Yoda.'
Homer Simpson

'A man in love is incomplete until he is married. Then he is finished.'
Zsa Zsa Gabor

'I have too much respect for the truth to drag it out on every occasion.'
Mark Twain

'Marriage is our last best chance to grow up.'
Joseph Barth

'That's the thing with love, it's going to be wrong until it's right.'
T.S.Elliot

ACKNOWLEDGEMENTS

Eliza for adding her creative magic, Rob Metcalfe for steering me to 'the first modern book on the wedding speech', Eli Goldstone for lending the voice of a true poet, Laura for not allowing me to settle for second best, Sam Jackson for challenging me to create a 'category killer', Hannah for keeping me real, and my editor Morwenna Loughman for her constant encouragement.

DESIGN TEAM

Our aim was to create a book in which the look and feel captured the enjoyment and fun of speaking at a wedding, and the joie de vivre of the occasion.

Sandra Salter's brilliant and witty illustrations and Jim Salter's superb art direction are so much more than the icing on the cake! www.saltysstudio.com

Notes

Cheers

Na zdravi

तरङ्ग

Chinchín!

hooray!